Festivals *of the* *World*

PHILIPPINES

Gareth Stevens Publishing
MILWAUKEE

Written by
LUNITA MENDOZA

Edited by
AUDREY LIM

Designed by
LYNN CHIN

Picture research by
SUSAN JANE MANUEL

First published in North America in 1999 by
Gareth Stevens Publishing
1555 North RiverCenter Drive, Suite 201
Milwaukee, Wisconsin 53212 USA

For a free color catalog describing Gareth
Stevens' list of high-quality books and multimedia
programs, call
1-800-542-2595 (USA)
or 1-800-461-9120 (Canada).
Gareth Stevens Publishing's Fax: (414) 225-0377.
See our catalog, too, on the World Wide Web:
http://gsinc.com

© **TIMES EDITIONS PTE LTD 1999**
Originated and designed by
Times Books International
an imprint of Times Editions Pte Ltd
Times Centre, 1 New Industrial Road
Singapore 536196
Printed in Singapore

Library of Congress Cataloging-in-Publication Data:
Mendoza, Lunita.
Philippines / by Lunita Mendoza.
p. cm.—(Festivals of the world)
Includes bibliographical references and index.
Summary: Describes how the culture of the
Philippines is reflected in its many festivals and
celebrations, including Ati-Atihan, Moriones,
and Christmas.
ISBN 0-8368-2025-8 (lib. bdg.)
1. Festivals—Philippines—Juvenile literature.
2. Philippines—Social life and customs—Juvenile
literature. [1. Festivals—Philippines.
2. Holidays—Philippines. 3. Philippines—Social
life and customs.] I. Title. II. Series.
GT4881.M46   1999
394.269599—dc21   98-37438

1 2 3 4 5 6 7 8 9 03 02 01 00 99

CONTENTS

It's Festival Time . . .

Filipinos love to have fun, and it is obvious in the way they celebrate *fiestas* [fee-EST-as] and religious festivals. Fiestas usually feature music, dancing, and feasts, and they are considered special opportunities for people to extend hospitality and friendship to one another. Come see how farmers honor their patron saint, *San Isidro Labrador* [SUN e-see-DRAW lab-bra-DOOR]. Watch party-goers celebrate *Ati-Atihan* [ah-TI ah-ti-HAN]. Make a Christmas **parol** [pa-ROOL]! It's festival time in the Philippines . . .

WHERE ARE THE PHILIPPINES?

The islands of the Philippines form the world's second largest **archipelago** after Indonesia. There are three main island groups: Luzon, the Visayas, and Mindanao. Situated in the Pacific between the South China Sea and the Philippine Sea, its neighbors are Taiwan to the north, Malaysia to the southwest, and Vietnam to the west.

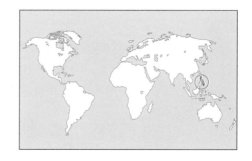

Participants of Ati-Atihan are colorfully dressed to join in the celebrations.

Who are the Filipinos?

The original inhabitants of the Philippines came from different parts of Asia, including Indonesia, China, Japan, and India. In the 16th century, the Philippines became a Spanish colony, and Christianity was introduced to the country. In 1898, the islands were ceded to the United States. The Philippines became independent in 1946, after World War II. Today, the majority of Filipinos are Christians, while the larger minority groups are Muslims and pagan hill tribes.

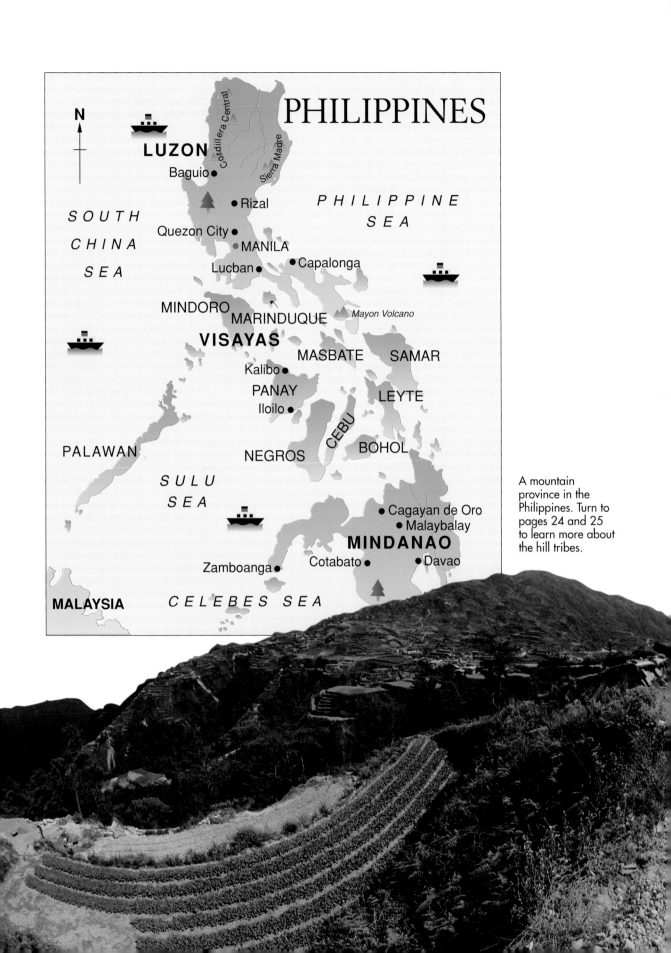

PHILIPPINES

LUZON

Cordillera Central

Sierra Madre

Baguio •

• Rizal

PHILIPPINE SEA

Quezon City •

• MANILA

Lucban •

• Capalonga

MINDORO

MARINDUQUE

Mayon Volcano

VISAYAS

MASBATE

SAMAR

Kalibo •

SOUTH CHINA SEA

PANAY

Iloilo •

LEYTE

CEBU

PALAWAN

NEGROS

BOHOL

SULU SEA

• Cagayan de Oro

• Malaybalay

MINDANAO

Zamboanga •

Cotabato •

• Davao

MALAYSIA

CELEBES SEA

A mountain province in the Philippines. Turn to pages 24 and 25 to learn more about the hill tribes.

WHEN'S THE FIESTA?

RELIGIOUS CELEBRATIONS

✪ **FEAST OF THE THREE KINGS**
✪ **ATI-ATIHAN**
✪ **HOLY WEEK**
✪ **ANTIPOLO PILGRIMAGE**—A pilgrimage is made every year to the Shrine of Our Lady of Peace and Good Voyage in Antipolo, Rizal. Spanish sailors believed the image of the Blessed Mother could keep them safe on trips, so they brought it with them to the Philippines.
✪ **BLACK NAZARENE FESTIVAL**—Pilgrims come to Capalonga to pay homage to the town's patron saint, the Black Nazarene. They pray for a year of prosperity and profitable business.
✪ **CARABAO FESTIVAL**
✪ **MAYOHAN SA TAYABAS**
✪ **CHRISTMAS**

TRIBAL FESTIVALS

✪ **KALIBONGAN FESTIVAL**—One of the most colorful festivals in the Philippines, in which the different tribes of Cotabato participate in a tribal dance contest.
✪ **T'BOLI FESTIVAL**—A festival to inspire the T'boli tribe to recapture their magnificent past, known as *Lem-Lunay* [lamb-LOO-nai]. This celebration is held at Lake Sebu in South Cotabato.

NATIONAL CELEBRATIONS

- ✪ **NEW YEAR'S DAY**
- ✪ **LABOR DAY**—Workers in the Philippines enjoy a holiday held in their honor.
- ✪ **INDEPENDENCE DAY**
- ✪ **NATIONAL HEROES' DAY**—This holiday commemorates Philippines' heroes who died during both World Wars.
- ✪ **ALL SAINTS' DAY**—People visit cemeteries to remember those who have passed away and to say prayers for them.
- ✪ **BONIFACIO DAY**—This holiday honors Andre Bonifacio, whom Filipinos regard as a hero of the Philippines' revolt against Spain.

Ati-Atihan is a terrific celebration. Turn to page 8 to see the action!

CULTURAL FESTIVALS

- ✪ **JEEPNEY KING FESTIVAL**—The *jeepney* [JEEP-knee] driver is honored in Manila. Celebrations include exhibitions of colorful jeepneys and fiesta caravans.
- ✪ **GREAT SIBIDAN FESTIVAL**—As part of the festivities, 40 fishermen participate in a boat race.
- ✪ **KAGAYHAAN FIESTA**—Held once a year in Cagayan de Oro city, this celebration showcases the dances and music of regional ethnic groups.
- ✪ **KAAMULAN**—Various ethnic groups in Malaybalay perform their music and dances.

ATI-ATIHAN

The Santo Niño is honored during Ati-Atihan.

C elebrated during January by people living in the Visayas, Ati-Atihan is a mixture of both pagan and Christian elements. The lively festivities last three days.

In honor of the Christ Child

Ati-Atihan was originally a pagan festival. Missionaries gradually added Christian meaning. Today, Ati-Atihan is celebrated in honor of the Christ Child, the *Santo Niño* [SUN-toh NIN-yoh].

Three days of parades lead up to the main procession that starts in church on Sunday afternoon. The parades are colorful and vibrant, much like the Mardi Gras carnival in Brazil.

Listen to a story

No one is certain how Ati-Atihan started. One legend, however, says it dates back to the year 1212, when 10 *datus* [DA-toos], or patriarchal chiefs, and their companions fled from a tyrannical sultan in Sabah, Borneo, and landed on the island of Panay. Their leader, Datu Puti, traded with the chief of Panay, an Ati named Marikudo.

Datu Puti exchanged gold and other gifts in return for the coastal lowlands. The bargain was sealed with a great feast and dancing, during which the Borneans blackened their faces with soot to resemble the dark-skinned Atis. Modern day celebrants of Ati-Atihan paint their faces and bodies with black soot to remember the Atis. Today, the Atis are a minority.

Brightly colored costumes are all part of the festive cheer during Ati-Atihan.

9

Blackened faces and bright headdresses make a dramatic contrast.

The excitement builds

Ati-Atihan takes place at Kalibo in Panay in the second week of January, then at Ibajay and Makati one week later. To prepare for the festival, villagers make their own unique costumes and form groups to practice dances. Their costumes look either bizarre or regal. **Anticipation** builds up during the last few days of preparation and reaches an exciting climax on Friday, when the dancing and partying start.

Join in the fun!

No one remains a spectator at Ati-Atihan for long. Many travelers join in the celebration by painting their faces and wearing costumes. In Kalibo, besides being part of the procession, visitors also get to feast on the scrumptious food prepared by residents of the province.

Music is an important part of the celebration.

Hala, bira!

During Ati-Atihan, streets are filled with people singing and dancing in striking costumes. These costumes are usually brightly colored, with tall, impressive headdresses. Faces blackened with soot, parade participants move to the rhythm of drumbeats and the clanging sound of tin cans, crying *"Hala, bira* ! [ha-LAH bee-RAH]" which means "To strike a blow." School bands and orchestras add to the music, and revelers celebrate late into the night.

In stark contrast to the riotous festivities that happen throughout the three-day celebration, Ati-Atihan ends **somberly** with a procession on Sunday. Participants carry torches and, starting from their town churches, walk along the streets that outline their towns.

Think about this

The large central group of islands between Luzon and Mindanao is called the Visayas. It consists of six of the Philippines' 11 major islands and includes many other smaller islands. If you had the chance to live on an island, which island would you choose? Where is it located? Who would you bring along to live with you?

Energetic dancing is a crowd-pleaser during the festivities.

LENT AND MORIONES

L ent is a time when Catholics remember the crucifixion and resurrection of Jesus Christ. During the Lenten season, numerous Passion Plays are performed as part of the celebrations. People flock to Marinduque to watch the *moriones* [mor-ree-YUN-nes] in a spectacular reenactment of the legend of Longinus.

Put on your mask and come with me to search for Longinus.

Holy Week

The start of Holy Week is Palm Sunday. Catholics carry palm leaves, known as *palaspas* [pa-las-PASS], to church for the priest to bless. Catholics also celebrate Maundy Thursday, attending church services and watching Passion Plays. In one practice called *visita iglesia* [vi-si-TA e-gla-SHEE-ya], Catholics try to visit as many churches as they can. On Good Friday, believers in certain areas, such as Manila, San Fernando in Oamoanga Province, and Antipolo in Rizal Province, reenact the sufferings and death of Christ on the Cross. Although Good Friday is a somber time, Easter Sunday is a joyful occasion that starts with **salubongs** [SA-loo-bongs], or dawn processions. In these processions, statues representing the Risen Christ and the Grieving Mother are carried to meet at an appointed place.

Opposite: Fervent participants of the Lenten rites during Holy Week.

After the play is over, those who perform as moriones relax.

Masks and legends

As part of Easter celebrations, Marinduque townspeople reenact the Longinus legend based on the Gospel of Saint John. The legend remembers Longinus, the Roman legionnaire who became a Christian.

Some participants in the performance play moriones, or Roman soldiers, by wearing masks and costumes. A typical morion mask is oversized and made from coral wood painted pink or red. It has large eyes, a full black beard, and an open mouth. The mask is topped with a colorful helmet, called *turbante* [tour-BAN-teh]. The wearer of the mask carves it himself. The participant's identity is kept secret because performing as a moriones is meant to be a sacrifice. The moriones outfit looks like the uniform Roman legionnaires used to wear. In performing the story of "Longinus according to Saint John," the town forms the stage.

This mask conceals a performer's identity.

14

All about Longinus

During the reenactment, children wear costumes and are part of the group that chases Longinus.

Catholics believe Longinus was the Roman soldier who speared Christ's side when He was hanging on the Cross. Longinus was blind in one eye, but he regained his vision when Christ's blood dropped on his eye. Longinus then believed in Christ and told others what had happened. His faith, however, turned his fellow soldiers against him. They arrested him on Easter Sunday and beheaded him.

During the reenactment, moriones chase Longinus for a long time. He is caught three times. He also escapes three times. When the moriones catch Longinus a fourth time, they march him to the scaffold, led by a brass band. After Longinus bravely confirms his faith in Christ, he is beheaded. His body is placed on a stretcher, paraded around town, and taken to a church.

Think about this

How do you think the moriones got their name? Some people believe the name might have come from the "morion," a high-crested helmet with turned-up edges used by Spanish conquistadors. Others think the name came from Governor General Domingo Moriones, who ruled the Philippines from 1877 to 1880. Which do you think is a more convincing explanation?

In Honor of San Isidro Labrador

San Isidro Labrador is the patron saint of farmers in the Philippines. Many festivals, such as the **Carabao** [KAH-rah-bow] Festival and *Pahiyas* [pah-HEE-yas], are held to honor this saint and give thanks for plentiful harvests. Good harvests are important because the Philippines has primarily an **agricultural economy**. Main crops include rice, corn, sugarcane, and coconuts. Festivals occur in May, the month of rest between one season's harvest and the next season's planting. Everyone, not just farmers, enjoys these celebrations, and they take a break from work to revel in the festivities.

At the Carabao Festival, people pay tribute to the water buffalo.

The Carabao Festival

Beginning on May 14th, people in Pulilan of Bulacan Province, San Isidor in Nueva Ecija Province, and Angono in Rizal Province celebrate for two days. On the first day, farmers pay tribute to water buffalos, known as carabaos. These animals are very important to farmers because they help till the land. Farmers brush their water buffalos' skin until it is sleek and shiny. Then, these creatures are decorated with ribbons and attached to carts. In the afternoon, farmers lead their water buffalos to the church square to be part of a procession. At the church, the buffalos kneel for their blessings! On the second day, water buffalos compete in friendly races.

Above: A water buffalo kneels in the midst of spectators.

This child is riding a water buffalo in a festival procession.

Besides being used as decorations, colorful palm hats are hung as offerings to San Isidro Labrador.

Pahiyas

Pahiyas is the time when people in Lucban give thanks to San Isidro Labrador for a good harvest. *Pahiyas* means "decor," and, on May 15th, the fronts of houses are elaborately adorned with brightly colored rice wafers, called **kiping** [kee-PING], a type of rice dough made from a traditional recipe. When the festival is over, these wafers are cooked and eaten as rice chips. Fruits, grain, vegetables, and even woven palm hats are used as decorations! In the afternoon, San Isidro Labrador's image is carried across town in a procession to assure farmers of more bountiful harvests in forthcoming seasons.

Men carrying the image of San Isidro Labrador in a procession.

18

Fiestas and saints

Fiestas were introduced to the Philippines when it became a Spanish colony and have been used by Filipinos in particular regions to honor their patron saints. Because of the importance of agriculture in their lives, these people felt they needed divine protection to ensure good harvests. Such fiestas also were important because they gave people a chance to take a break from daily work routines. During these celebrations, local residents enjoyed music, dancing, and drama presentations.

Honoring saints today

Today's fiestas are still primarily religious. Even pagan hill tribe fiestas contain Christian elements as a result of contact with Christian missionaries. Since every community holds an annual fiesta on the feast day of its patron saint, there is always a fiesta happening somewhere. Most fiestas are strictly local celebrations. People attend church services and enjoy colorful street decorations in villages and city districts.

Celebrations, such as Pahiyas, are a time for children to enjoy themselves and take a break from school.

Think about this

Decorations for Pahiyas are always elaborate and extensive. If the harvest has been abundant, a less extravagant display would mean being ungrateful to San Isidro Labrador. If, however, the harvest was not as good as expected, these displays serve as a reminder to the saint to do more for the farmers the next season!

CHRISTMAS

Christmas celebrations in the Philippines are among the longest in the world. They start on December 16th and end on the first Sunday of January the following year. December 16th is the start of **simbang gabi** [sim-BANG ga-bee], nine days of masses held at around four o'clock each morning. Mass is usually followed by a breakfast of local delicacies at stalls set up in the churchyard. On Christmas Eve, a midnight mass is followed by the traditional *noche buena* [noh-CHAY BUAY-nah], or midnight supper. Throughout the Christmas season, dining tables are usually filled with local dishes and fruits.

Christmas is a happy time for children, especially when they exchange gifts!

People love to have Christmas parties where they can dance.

Leading up to Christmas

The days leading up to Christmas are very hectic, especially in Manila. About 12 million residents hustle and bustle to do last-minute shopping, especially at Quinta Market in downtown Quiapo, located in the city of Manila. Christmas preparations include baking fruitcakes and soaking them in brandy for flavor. Cooked chickens are stuffed in advance and frozen. **Confectioners** are especially busy. They need to have enough sweets for the nation's feasting and gift-giving. One popular sweet treat is *turrones* [too-ROW-nes], which are made from glutinous rice, coconut milk, and sugar. Clearly, food plays an important part in the Filipino Christmas.

Caroling adds to the festive cheer. These children are dressed and ready to start caroling.

The end of the season

The Feast of the Three Kings honors the three wise men who journeyed to Bethlehem in search of the Christ Child. Held on the first Sunday in January, this holiday marks the official end of the Christmas season and is the last day for giving gifts. Children receive presents symbolizing the gold, myrrh, and frankincense given to the Infant Jesus by the three wise men. Lanterns shaped like stars are hung from windows and doorways, representing the star the wise men followed to Bethlehem. Some provinces celebrate by reenacting the wise men's journey.

Opposite: Shopping centers usually have lavishly decorated trees at Christmastime.

Performers reenact the nativity as part of Christmas celebrations.

Think about this

In the Philippines, Christmas is a time when people try to strengthen family bonds. They usually gather in the homes of the oldest family members and exchange gifts. Children visiting their relatives are given money and gifts, known as *aguinaldo* [ah-gee-NAL-doh].

RICE FESTIVALS

A member of the Ifugao tribe.

Both people who live in the mountains and people who stay on the lowlands enjoy rice as their main food. Growing rice, however, is much more difficult in the mountains, especially in the **craggy** hills of Northern Luzon.

Planting and harvesting rice

People living in the mountains, such as the Ifugao, have very little land for raising crops, so they need to plant and harvest twice a year. The *chinacon* [CHEE-na-kon], or first crop, is grown from January to July, and the *pak ang* [PAK ang], or second crop, is grown from August to December. Mountain people face many difficulties cultivating rice, and they believe they need special help from the supernatural to raise successful crops. For the mountain people, giving thanks for a successful rice harvest is a great time to celebrate.

A rice harvest dance in progress.

Cañao

Cañaos [KAH-neows] are prestige feasts people use as occasions to celebrate. Cañaos must reflect the giver's status in the community. Status in a community is measured by the number of livestock a family owns and the size of its rice fields. Wealthy Bontocs, Ifugaos, and Kalingas traditionally offer this feast, at least once a year, to give thanks for a bountiful harvest. During a cañao, people dance, eat, and drink rice wine day and night.

Appey

Bontocs celebrate *Appey* [UP-pay] to give thanks for a successful rice harvest. Appey lasts three days and contains both Christian and pagan influences. In seeking a fruitful harvest, some Bontoc farming families set up small wooden crosses, which have been blessed by priests, in their fields and offer prayers. Other families prefer to set up *paloke* [pa-LOW-kay], the plant sacred to the pagan god, Lumawig. Appey celebrants feast on chicken and pork.

25

THINGS FOR YOU TO DO

Filipinos enjoy a good fiesta any time, because it is an opportunity to sing and dance. There are many different types of dances in the Philippines, some harder than others. Read on to learn more!

Learn a dance

Filipino dances often feature Malay and Spanish styles. Popular Spanish dances at fiestas include the *jota* [HO-tah] and *curacha* [koo-RAH-chah]. Native dances revolve around themes, such as nature, a warrior's victory, courtship, or even death. One dance using bamboo poles, called the *tinikling* [tee-NICK-ling], has movements that mimic the quickness of birds as they move. A folk dance with Muslim roots, called the *singkil* [SING-kil], is performed by Philippine women who move deftly and gracefully between criss-crossed bamboo poles while performing complicated movements with fans.

To enjoy Filipino dances yourself, you can easily use two jump ropes in place of bamboo poles. Ask some friends to hold the ends of the ropes apart, wide enough for you to stand between them. As your friends bring the ropes together, step out to the right and lift your left foot. As they move the ropes apart, step back between the ropes with one foot on the floor at a time. Repeat the same movements on the left side. Wasn't that easy? Practice and see who can dance the fastest!

Sing a Filipino song!

Singing songs at fiestas always adds to the festive cheer. Practice this song about a family going fishing. Both *bugaong* [BU-ga-ong] and *katambak* [ka-TAM-bak] are types of fish. If you have a friend who can play the piano, the two of you can rehearse together and entertain your family and friends!

Si nanay, si tatay

Fish-ing one day at sea Mom and Dad feel a bite, But it's not a bu-ga-ong It's a ka-tam-bak! a ka-tam-bak!

Si na-nay, si ta-tay Na-ma-sol sa da-gat, Pag-ku-bit bu-ga-ong Pag-bi-ra ka-tam-bak! -ra ka-tam-bak!

Things to look for in your library

Best of the Islands—A to Z. (Philippine Department of Tourism, 1996).

Children of the Philippines. World's Children (series). Sheila Kinkade (Carolrhoda Books Inc., 1996).

Christmas in the Philippines. Cheryl Enderlein (Franklin Watts, 1997).

Colors of the Islands Philippines. (Philippine Department of Tourism, 1993).

Filipino Americans. Footsteps to America (series). Alexandra Bandon (New Discovery Books, 1993).

The Philippines: Pacific Crossroads. Taking Part Books (series). Margaret W. Sullivan and Mike Downey (Dillon Press, 1998).

MAKE A PAROL

The most popular symbol of Christmas in the Philippines is the parol. It represents the blessed star of Bethlehem. For Filipinos, not having a parol as a decoration makes Christmas somewhat incomplete. The parol's size depends on where it will be hung. A very large parol is usually used for high-rise buildings. For regular houses, parols are smaller.

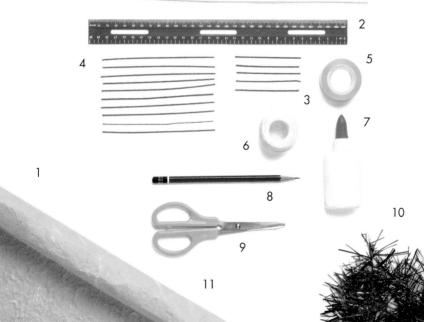

You will need:

1. Two 32-inch (80-cm) bamboo strips
2. A ruler
3. Five 3-inch (7.5-cm) wire strips
4. Ten 7-inch (17.5-cm) wire strips
5. Tape
6. Thread
7. Glue
8. A pencil
9. Scissors
10. Tinsel
11. Colorful paper 24" x 24" (60 x 60 cm)

1 Use thread to tie the ends of each bamboo strip together, forming two circles.

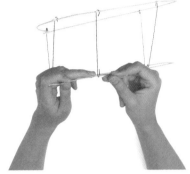

2 Use the two circles and five of the 7-inch (17.5-cm) wire strips to make a frame by twisting the ends of each wire strip around the bamboo circles as shown.

3 Fold the colorful paper in half. Draw the shape of a five-pointed star and cut it out. You will have two stars.

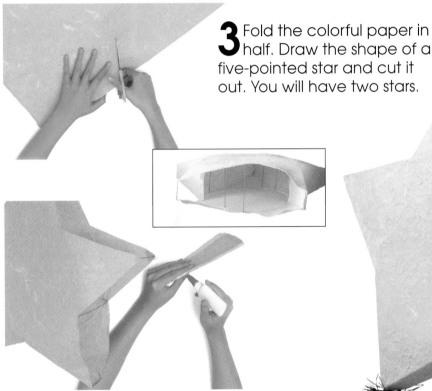

4 Glue one star to each side of the circular frame. Attach the other five 7-inch (17.5-cm) wires to the five points where the angles of the star touch the wire frame. Attach the five 3-inch (7.5-cm) wires to the tips of the star so the star bulges. Tie some thread to one of these wires. Glue on pieces of paper to cover the frame. Attach tinsel to the two bottom points of the star.

MAKE HALO HALO

Filipinos love sweet desserts, and a particularly easy one to make is *halo halo* [ha-LOW ha-LOW], which means "mix mix." This refreshing sweet treat contains an interesting variety of ingredients. Try it on a hot day to cool down! This recipe makes two servings.

1 Mix together all ingredients except the evaporated milk, the sugar, and the crushed ice.

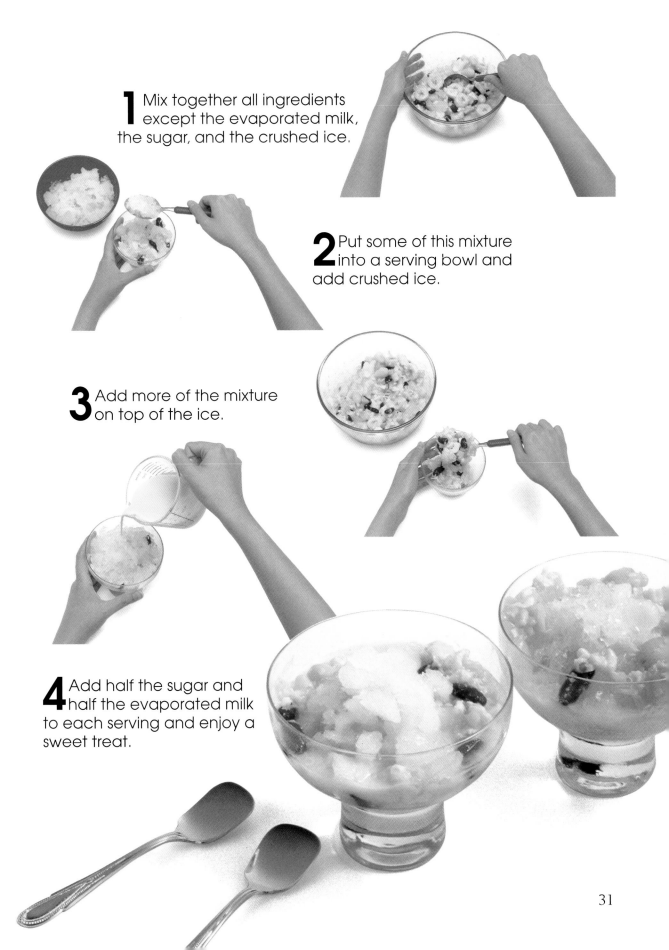

2 Put some of this mixture into a serving bowl and add crushed ice.

3 Add more of the mixture on top of the ice.

4 Add half the sugar and half the evaporated milk to each serving and enjoy a sweet treat.

Glossary

agricultural economy, 16	A type of economic system in which agricultural products form the bulk of a country's resources and products.
aguinaldo, 23	Money and gifts given to children by relatives at Christmas.
anticipation, 10	Expectation of what is to come.
archipelago, 4	A group of many scattered islands.
carabao, 16	Water buffalo.
confectioners, 21	People who make or sell candy and other kinds of sweets.
craggy, 24	Hilly and rocky.
halo halo, 30	A refreshing dessert made with a sweetened combination of fruits and vegetables.
kiping, 18	Brightly colored rice wafers used to decorate the fronts of houses during Pahiyas.
parol, 3	Five-pointed lantern used as a special Christmas decoration.
salubongs, 12	Dawn processions on Easter Sunday.
simbang gabi, 20	Nine days of early dawn masses starting on December 16th.
somberly, 11	Solemnly and with great seriousness.

Index

Picture credits
Bes Stock: 1, 8, 9, 10 (both), 13, 14 (bottom), 15, 16, 17 (both), 18 (both), 19, 25; Chris Davis: 7 (top), 26; Haga Library: 3 (bottom), 6, 11, 28; The Hutchison Library: 14 (top); Michael Macintyre: 12; Photobank Photolibrary/Singapore: 2, 7 (bottom); Pietro Scòzzari: 3 (top); George Tapan: 20, 21 (both), 22, 23; Topham Picturepoint: 4, 5, 24

Digital scanning by
Superskill Graphics Pte Ltd